75 Self-Love and Positive Affirmations with
Beautiful Floral
Arrangements
Coloring BooK

Belongs to:

Name: ....

Address: ....

Pnone No: ....

Copyright©Reigndrop LLC
All rights reserved

Dear customers,

Thank you for choosing this coloring book to be the choice of your self-love affirmations coloring journey. I hope you get the most out of it.

Below are my suggestions on how to use this coloring book. However, it is up to you how you want to use it. Ultimately, it is YOU who creates your reality.

1. Begin with setting the intention that you want to connect to the message that you are about to color. Energy flows to where your intention goes.
2. Take deep breaths to settle your energy. Say the affirmation out loud or to yourself and believe in it. Remember, you are a creator of your own life!
3. While you are coloring, feel the affirmation in your heart. Don't think it, no conversation, no dialogue, just feel it. Get high on the affirmation. You are limitless!
4. Be in the present moment by feeling the movement of your hand or focusing on the color that is coming out. This is your space, relax and enjoy it.

Are you enjoying the coloring books?
Don't forget to give me feedback.
If you would like more, I am happy to give you some more coloring pages.
Send me an email at *magicalpencil.us@gmail.com*

Sincerely,
Magical Pencil

Color Test Page

I am Thankful

I am loved

I am Important

I am Fearless

I am at Peace

I am Healthy

I can do Hard Things

My Heart
Receives only Love

I Let Go
of
Self Doubts

I let go of toxic people

I Love Myself

I create my life path

My creativity creates abundance

I Don't give up Easily

Made in the USA
Columbia, SC
12 September 2022

67062627R00085